I'm an
ASTRONOMER
now!

Who Me? series co-editors: David A. Weintraub, Professor of Astronomy, of History, and of Communication of Science and Technology, College of Arts & Science, Vanderbilt University; Ann Neely, Professor Emerita of the Practice of Education, Peabody College of Education and Human Development, Vanderbilt University; and Kevin Johnson, Professor of Biomedical Informatics and of Pediatrics, Vanderbilt University Medical Center

Published by

WS Education, an imprint of

World Scientific Publishing Co. Pte. Ltd.

5 Toh Tuck Link, Singapore 596224

USA office: 27 Warren Street, Suite 401-402, Hackensack, NJ 07601

UK office: 57 Shelton Street, Covent Garden, London WC2H 9HE

British Library Cataloguing-in-Publication Data

A catalogue record for this book is available from the British Library.

Who Me? — Vol. 1
I'M AN ASTRONOMER NOW!

Copyright 2021 by World Scientific Publishing Co. Pte. Ltd.

ISBN 978-981-124-023-2 (hardcover)
ISBN 978-981-124-024-9 (ebook for institutions)
ISBN 978-981-124-025-6 (ebook for individuals)

Desk Editor: Daniele Lee

Printed in Singapore

Front cover, P4: David Dubois, Vanderbilt University; **P6, 8 (top L&R), 10, 12, 14, 31 (bottom), 36 (top)**: Keivan Stassun; **P8** (bottom): Ens. Darin K. Russell; **P9, 22, 24, 26, 28, 36 (bottom), P37**: NASA; **P13 (from top down)**: Sarah Crosby/Daily Hampshire Gazette, Modesto Bee/John Holland; **P16**: coconutbaby/Shutterstock.com; **P17 (top)**: Artur Balytskyi/Shutterstock.com; **P17, 21, 25 (right), 33**: Wikipedia Commons; **P19 (from top down)**: Jonatan Svensson Glad, L. Calçada/freegreatpicture.com, Powerhauer; **P20**: ESO; **P23**: ESA; **P29 (from top down)**: Steve Sickels Photography, M. Kornmesser; **P30**: Akira Fiji/David Malin Images; **P31**: CTIO/NOIRLab/NSF/AURA/P. Marenfeld; **P32, 34, 35**: Creative Services, Vanderbilt University

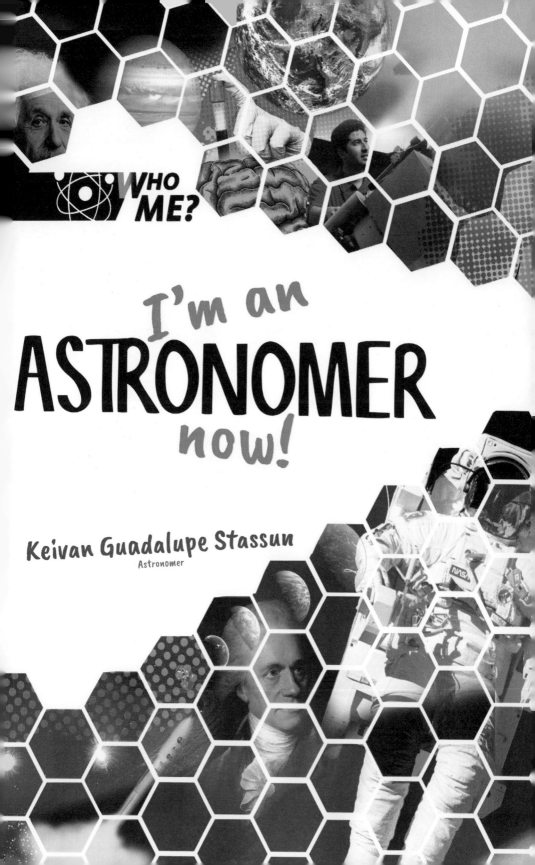

WHO ME?

I'm an ASTRONOMER now!

Keivan Guadalupe Stassun

Astronomer

Table of contents

Keivan Stassun using the Dyer Observatory Telescope at Vanderbilt University.

1 I Want to Become an Astronomer

My name is Keivan. In Persian, it means the planet Saturn. Persian is the language of my father, whom I never knew. I often wonder if I was destined to be an **astronomer** learning about **planets**.

Growing up in California, I wanted to become an **astronaut**. I wanted to soar above the Earth and travel to Mars!

I wanted to soar above the Earth and travel to Mars!

Keivan at age 3

Keivan as a
college student

I thought the way to achieve that goal was to become a pilot in the Navy. If I learned how to fly airplanes, then I could learn how to command a spaceship.

But along the way, I decided to become an astronomer. I would work to unravel some of the mysteries of the universe. In order to do that, I needed to learn about physics, chemistry and mathematics.

Navy pilots Andy Muller (left) and Bill Sizemore (right) walk back to the hanger after a training mission in 2004 at Naval Air Station New Orleans.

Astronaut Bruce McCandless II is using a Manned Maneuvering Unit outside Space Shuttle Challenger in 1984. McCandless attended the United States Naval Academy. He then became a Navy Aviator. He flew planes off of aircraft carriers. Then he became an astronaut in 1966 and flew in space as a mission specialist on two space shuttle missions.

First, I had to graduate from high school. Then I went to college. Once there, I studied hard. I learned even more about physics and mathematics. I also learned how to program computers. From what I learned in college, I now had a solid background. I was ready to pursue my dream of becoming a scientist who discovers new things about the universe.

Keivan gives the valedictory address when he graduates from college in 1994.

2 Goals and Gravity

I was inspired by my mother to study hard in school, beginning at a young age. My mother grew up in a small village near Guadalajara, Mexico. There, she did not get a very good education. However, she understood that a great education opens doors to a world of opportunities. She was determined to make sure her son received a good education. She made the courageous journey to the United States when she was 20 years old. A few years later, I was born in Los Angeles, California.

Her goal was to become a United States citizen. She wanted to give me a chance to get a good education and the opportunity to achieve my own goals.

When I was young, my mother worked cleaning houses. We were very poor, but she was proud and strong. She worked very hard. In order to get by, we received assistance from the government in the form of food stamps and welfare checks.

While working and sending me to school, my mother studied for years. Although she was too old to attend high school, she eventually passed a test from the State of California and graduated.

Keivan, age four,
is waving the American flag with his
mother on the day she became a
United States citizen.

An English-as-a-Second-Language tutor teaches an immigrant from Senegal facts about each state in the United States. Knowing this information is required for the United States citizenship test.

Now she was a high school graduate! She studied even more. Then she passed her United States citizenship test and became an American citizen, like me! If my mother could do all of this, then I was determined to work just as hard to achieve my goals and to make her as proud of me as I am of her.

A new American citizen takes the citizenship oath at a ceremony in Modesto, California, on Monday, July 10, 2017.

Keivan, standing with his mother and stepfather, celebrates finishing graduate school.

An astronomer

I graduated from high school and began college at age 18. At the University of California, Berkeley, I began my studies in astronomy and fell in love with stars. That's when I decided I wanted to be a scientist who discovered new things about **stars**. Now I had my own goal — I wanted to be an astronomer.

Once I had the skills in math and physics to understand stars, I discovered that a single property of stars determines almost everything about them. This property is the total amount of matter in the star. Astronomers call this property **mass**. Every object in the universe, from a tiny grain of sand to the entire Earth, has mass. The Earth has an enormous amount of mass, so it is hard to move, while a grain of sand has a tiny mass, so it is easy to move.

The mass of a star is very important. It is the source of energy for a star and it affects the strength of the force we call **gravity**. A force makes objects speed up or slow down or change the direction in which they are moving. Gravity always pulls things towards other things. Gravity never pushes things apart. This is why the force of gravity on Earth pulls objects down towards the ground.

In our everyday lives, we experience gravity pulling us down towards the surface of the Earth. The Earth, however, is round. People on opposite sides of the Earth are all being pulled down. In this case, the direction we call down actually means towards the center of the Earth.

All objects have mass; therefore, all objects exert a gravitational pull on all other objects. The strength of that gravitational pull depends on the masses of both objects. It also depends on how far apart they are. If the masses are big, the gravitational pull is strong. If the masses are small, the gravitational pull is weak.

Similarly, if the two objects, for example, a planet and a star, are close together, the gravitational attraction of each for the other is greater than if the planet and star are far apart.

Apples fall down toward the ground because the force of gravity pulls the Earth and the apple toward each other. Because the Earth is so big, we think the Earth doesn't move, while the apple falls down. However, if the apple contained as much mass as the Earth, we would see them both move toward each other.

Did You Know?

GRAVITATION

The Earth pulls things toward the center of the Earth. In fact, the direction we call 'down' is determined by the direction in which objects are pulled by the Earth's gravity.

Energy can be stored in many ways on Earth and in the universe. The mass of a star is one of these ways in which energy is stored.

Albert Einstein discovered that mass is equivalent to energy. He expressed this idea in his famous equation $E = mc^2$ (pronounced 'E equals m c squared').

In this equation, E represents energy, m represents mass, and c represents the speed of light (186,000 miles per second).

17

On Earth, energy can be stored in many ways. Batteries, lumps of coal, and barrels of oil are different ways in which energy is stored. When we connect a battery to an **electric circuit**, we use the energy stored in the battery. When we burn coal or oil, we extract the energy stored in these fossil fuels.

How can nature convert the energy stored in the form of mass into light or heat? The mass must be in an environment in which the temperature is ten million degrees or hotter. Also, the pressure must be enormous! One of the few places in the entire universe where these conditions exist are at the centers of stars. The Sun and all other stars get their power by converting mass to energy. This process is called **nuclear fusion**.

The fuel source for a star depends on the amount of mass it contains. Stars have large amounts of mass. Nevertheless, they will eventually run out of fuel. The Sun, for example, has a lifespan of ten billion years.

A big star has more fuel than a little star. Similarly, a large truck will have a larger fuel tank than a small car. Big stars are also brighter and hotter than small stars.

Batteries, oil and lumps of coal all store energy in the form of chemical bonds. We can extract and use the energy in batteries by attaching wires to both ends to create an electric circuit.

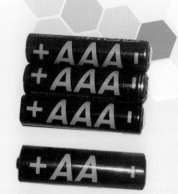

In order to get the energy out of coal, we must burn the coal. We then use the heat to generate electricity.

R136a1

blue dwarf

yellow dwarf (Sun-like)

red dwarf

Little stars are known as red dwarfs. The littlest red dwarf has about ten percent the mass of the yellow Sun.

The biggest blue dwarf stars can weigh eight to ten times more than the Sun. The star R136a1, which is one of the most massive stars known, is equal to more than 300 Suns put together.

R136a1 is in the center of the Tarantula Nebula in the galaxy known as the Large Magellanic Cloud.

To generate their heat and light, the big stars use up their fuel much faster than smaller stars do. In the same way, large trucks burn the gas in their fuel tanks at a much faster rate than do cars. As a result, big stars have shorter lifetimes as compared to small stars.

Because the masses of stars are so important for understanding how stars work, astronomers have worked very hard for nearly 200 years to find ways to measure stellar masses.

Isaac Newton is one of the greatest scientists who ever lived. He lived in the seventeenth century.

We can't take a star and put it on a scale in a laboratory on Earth! Instead, astronomers need another experimental method to measure stellar masses.

What do astronomers do? They use the law of gravity. More than 300 years ago, Isaac Newton was the first scientist to understand how gravity works. Gravity does not just pull things down toward the Earth's surface. Gravity is a force that pulls all objects toward all other objects. He wrote down an *equation*. That equation allows other scientists to calculate how strong the force of gravity is, in any situation.

Scientists can use Isaac Newton's equation for the force of gravity. They can make predictions about how objects like stars will behave. They can also calculate how fast a falling object will hit the ground. They can even predict how to make satellites *orbit* the Earth.

The force of gravity determines how fast a satellite travels as it orbits the Earth. Satellites in low-Earth orbits move quickly. Satellites in high-Earth orbits move slowly. The International Space Station (shown here) orbits at a height of between 205 and 270 miles above the surface of the Earth. It moves at an average speed of just under 5 miles per second. This speed is the same as 18,000 miles per hour. At this height, it completes one orbit around the Earth in only 1.5 hours.

Astronomers can measure the mass of the Earth by watching a satellite in *orbit*.

We can also use the law of gravity to measure the mass of the Sun. In order to do this, we measure the orbital period of the Earth (1 year) and the distance of the Earth from the center of the Sun (93 million miles).

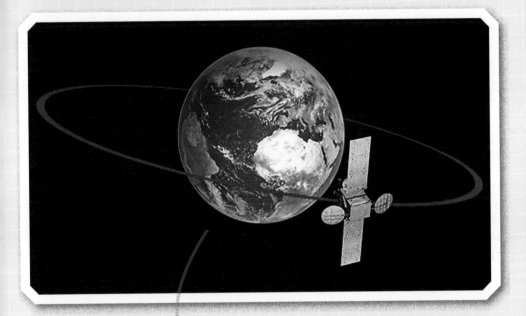

Did You Know?

To calculate the mass of the Earth, we need to measure two things. First, we measure how much time the satellite needs to complete one orbit. This length of time is called the orbital period. Second, we measure the height of the satellite above the ground. That height added to the distance from the surface to the center of the Earth is the size of the orbit.

The Sun's mass is much larger than the Earth's. The mass of the Sun is equivalent to 300,000 Earths!

Moon

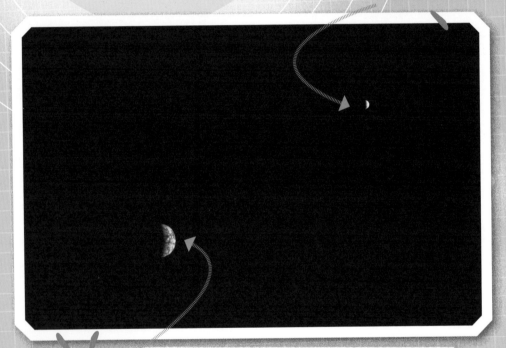

Earth

The Moon orbits the Earth at an average height of 236,000 miles. It completes one orbit in 27.3 days and moves at a speed of about 2,000 miles per hour. This image was acquired by a camera on NASA's Mars Reconnaissance Orbiter spacecraft. The picture shows the moon (located at the top right, shaped like a crescent) orbiting the Earth.

3 The Key: Binary Star Systems

My goal as an astronomer is to measure the masses of stars as accurately as possible. In space, one star can orbit another star. Together, two stars in orbit around each other are called a *binary star system*. Astronomers can use binary star systems to measure the masses of stars.

> An astronomer has to measure the masses of stars as accurately as possible

William Herschel was the first astronomer to discover and understand that two stars could orbit each other. He made this discovery more than 200 years ago. He coined the term binary stars to describe such a system.

A binary star system can have one blue star and one yellow star. The color of a star is determined by the temperature of its surface. Blue stars are extremely hot. Yellow stars, like the Sun, have intermediate temperatures. Red stars are the coolest.

Yellow star!

Astronomers use telescopes to watch binary stars as they travel in their orbits. They measure the position and the *velocity* of each star. They do this night after night, for a few days or weeks or years. From these measurements, astronomers determine the orbital periods of the stars. They also need to measure how far the stars are from the Sun and how far apart the two stars are from each other. With that information, they can calculate the number of miles that separates the two stars. Then astronomers use the law of gravity to calculate the masses of the stars!

Unfortunately, stars are very far away. For this reason, measuring their speeds and positions is very hard work. Alpha Centauri is the closest binary star system to the Earth. It is nearly four *light years* away. In the Alpha Centauri system, the smaller star is named Proxima Centauri. It is actually the closest star to the Earth and Sun.

To measure masses of stars, astronomers need to find very special binary star systems. They need stars in eclipsing binary systems. In an eclipsing binary system, one star will pass in front of the other. The star in front blocks out some or all of the light of the star in back. This is called an *eclipse*. It is just like a solar eclipse.

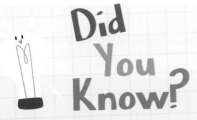

Did You Know?

What are light years? 'Light years' sound like an amount of time. It is actually a distance. If you could travel at the speed of light (186,000 miles per second) for one year, you would have traveled a distance of one light year. Since Alpha Centauri is four light years away, you would need four years to make the trip!

Spaceships in movies often travel faster than the speed of light. This can't actually happen. The speed of light is ten thousand times faster than the fastest rockets ever built. Our fastest rockets would need 50,000 years to get to Alpha Centauri! Space is a big place.

Humans won't be traveling to even the closest stars for a long, long time (except for in science fiction novels and movies).

The fastest rocket ever launched was the New Horizons mission to Pluto. It flew past Pluto in 2015. New Horizons had a top speed of about 10 miles per second. That speed is incredibly fast, but is also very slow compared to the speed of light.

A solar eclipse occurs when the Moon passes directly in between the Earth and the Sun and blocks out some or all of the light of the Sun. Solar eclipses last for only a few minutes.

Eclipses of stars in binary star systems often last for a few hours. Eclipsing binaries turn out to be very hard to find. I decided to try to find more of them because I think hard challenges in science are fun. Also, the reward for success would be learning important things about stars and the universe.

The Moon is blocking the light from the surface of the Sun during a total solar eclipse, as seen in Nashville, Tennessee in August, 2017. The light seen from the Sun during a total solar eclipse is from the Sun's outer layer called the chromosphere.

In an eclipsing binary star system, one of the stars will pass directly in front of the other star. When that happens, it temporarily blocks some of the light from the more distant star. During the eclipse, less light reaches Earth and our telescopes.

4 Doing Science and Making Discoveries

In 2006, I used telescopes in the country of Chile. Chile is in South America. My goal was to discover and study an eclipsing binary star system in the constellation Orion. I succeeded! I also used a tiny telescope in South Africa to study this binary system.

This picture shows a group of stars known as Orion, the hunter. The three bright stars in a line in the middle make up Orion's belt. The red giant star Betelgeuse, in the upper left, is one of Orion's shoulders. The blue giant named Rigel, in the lower right, is one of Orion's feet. The group of stars below the belt is Orion's dagger. The biggest, brightest spot of light in the dagger is not a star. It is a giant *interstellar cloud*, filled with thousands of newborn stars.

The mountainous region of northern Chile is one of the best places on Earth for astronomers. This region has dozens of telescopes. Some of the biggest telescopes ever built, including the Blanco telescope on Cerro Tololo, are there.

The KELT-South Telescope is co-owned by Ohio State University and Vanderbilt University. It is operated by the Cape Town Observatory in South Africa. KELT-South is remotely operated. This means that Keivan and his students can control the telescope from Tennessee using computers. They do not have to be on the mountain in South Africa when they use the telescope to study stars.

This drawing depicts two brown dwarfs in orbit around each other. Because brown dwarfs cool off as they get older, their colors will be red (not brown, despite their name).

We made many measurements of the two stars. We discovered that both stars were too small to be normal stars, but too big to be giant planets. Objects like these are known as **brown dwarfs**.

Unlike stars, brown dwarfs are not able to convert very much of their mass into energy. As a result, although brown dwarfs are very hot when they are born, they slowly cool down as they get older.

These pictures allow us to compare the size of Earth to the size of Jupiter. More than 300 Earths could fit inside Jupiter.

Did You Know?

How big are brown dwarfs? Jupiter is the biggest planet that orbits the Sun. If we could find 318 Earths and combine them together into one giant planet, that planet would have the mass of Jupiter.

What if you could take 55 Jupiters and put them together? You would have an object with as much mass as the big brown dwarf in this binary system. The little one is the equivalent of 35 Jupiters.

Astronomers like me will make more detailed measurements of the temperatures and brightnesses of these two brown dwarfs. Then we will be able to test our ideas for how tiny stars form and live.

In 2008, I discovered another binary star system. I thought that these two stars had the same mass and were born at the same time. They were like twins.

I needed to make more measurements to test my hypothesis. Our observations revealed a surprise. One of these stars is hotter than the other! If the stars had been twins, they would have had the same temperature.

Imagine two brothers born in a giant interstellar cloud. We could use our observations to determine whether they are twins or brothers of different ages.

In this binary star system, one of the stars is a small star surrounded by a dust cloud. The other star is a red giant.

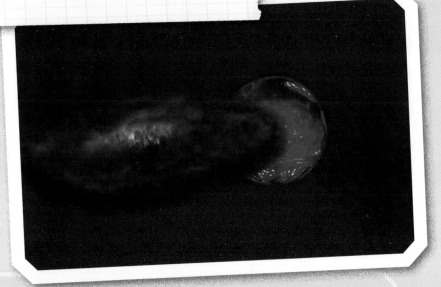

The fact that they have different temperatures means that they cannot be exactly the same age. They are brothers, one a little bit older and cooler, one a little bit younger and hotter than the other!

In 2016, I made another exciting discovery about binary stars. I helped set a world record for finding the binary star system with the longest eclipse.

In this system, the two stars need 69 years to complete their orbits. One of the stars is a red giant. The other star is surrounded by an enormous cloud of dust. Sometimes the star with the dust cloud passes in between the red giant star and the Earth. At that time, the light from the red giant star disappeared for almost 3.5 years.

Because of my knowledge about binary stars, I became part of a team that used a telescope in space called TESS to search for planets around other stars. TESS is an acronym for Transiting Exoplanet Survey Satellite. It has orbited Earth and studied other stars for three years already, and will probably continue to work until 2024.

Keivan with his wife Justine and sons Jaime and Emilio with their VIP passes. They were at Cape Canaveral in Florida on April 18, 2018, watching the launch of the SpaceX Falcon9 rocket. The Falcon9 carried TESS into orbit around the Earth.

TESS studied 400,000 of the brightest stars in the sky. My astronomer colleagues and I used the TESS data to discover almost 100 planets, including one orbiting the star named AU Microscopii. We might find more than 1,000 more *exoplanets* before we're done. We made these discoveries by looking for eclipses caused by planets passing in between the other stars and the Sun. Some of them are only a little bit bigger than the Earth.

Some of the exoplanets discovered by TESS are only a little bit larger than Earth.

TESS discovered a planet called AU Mic b. This planet is only 32 light-years from Earth, and it orbits the star AU Microscopii. AU Mic b is close enough that a future spaceship with people on board may someday travel there.

This planet is about 20 million years old. It is one of the youngest planets known to astronomers. The star pelts the planet with energetic eruptions, including powerful X-rays. As a result, life probably could not exist on AU Mic b. NASA decided to make a Spanish language version of the poster, which means my mom can enjoy my discoveries too.

These newly discovered exoplanets will help us learn more about how many planets exist around other stars. We will also discover how many of these exoplanets are similar to the Earth. Those exoplanets are called Earthlike exoplanets. Living things might even live in the oceans, on land, or in the atmosphere of one of these Earthlike exoplanets.

I will probably never become an astronaut, but I never gave up on my dream of learning about planets. Although I have never gone to outer space, I did become an astronomer and have spent my life learning about objects in space. In this way, I achieved part of my dream.

GLOSSARY

astronomer	a scientist who studies moons, planets, stars, galaxies and the universe
astronaut	a person who is the pilot or member of the crew of a spaceship and travels to outer space
binary star system	a star system with two stars that orbit each other
brown dwarf	an object that is bigger than a planet but smaller than a star
eclipse	an event that occurs when one object blocks the light of a second object
electric circuit	a loop of material that can conduct electricity from one place to another
equation	a mathematical expression that says that two things are equal
exoplanet	a planet that orbits a star that is not the Sun
gravity	the force that makes all objects with mass pull on all other objects with mass, that pulls things down toward the surface of Earth and makes planets orbit the Sun
light year	the distance that something would travel in one year if it could travel at the speed of light, equal to about six trillion miles
interstellar cloud	a region of outer space, in between the stars, where the density of gas and dust is greater than in other regions of outer space and where new stars are sometimes born
mass	a property of a body that measures how it resists a force that tries to change the speed and direction in which it moves

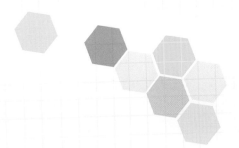

nuclear fusion	the process by which the nuclei of two atoms collide and fuse into a larger nucleus and by which mass is converted into energy deep inside stars
orbit	(noun) the curved path one object travels when the force of gravity causes it to travel around another object
orbit	(verb) to move around something else under the influence of the force of gravity
planet	an object that is much smaller than a star, that orbits a star, and that is big enough that the force of gravity shapes it so that it is round
star	an object that has enough mass to squeeze itself hard enough that it can turn mass into energy through the process of nuclear fusion
super Earth	a planet orbiting another star whose diameter and circumference are about three times bigger than those of Earth
orbital period	the length of time needed for one object in space to travel all the way around another object
TESS (Transiting Exoplanet Survey Satellite)	a satellite that NASA launched in 2018 that carries a telescope that astronomers use to search for planets around other stars
velocity	the speed at which something moves combined with knowledge about the direction in which it moves

Discussion Questions

1. Why do you think Keivan Stassun's mother thought that making sure her son received a better education than she was able to get was so important?

2. What school subjects do you think are most important for someone who wants to become an astronaut or an astronomer?

3. Rather than saying "gravity pulls me down," what words would you use to better explain the direction toward which gravity pulls you when you are standing on the surface of the Earth?

4. Why do you think astronomers are interested in discovering and learning about exoplanets?

5. If you could travel on a rocket to a star located only one light year from the Earth and Sun, how long do you think the trip would take? How long would a rocket trip take to go to the Moon? To Mars?

Additional Resources

You can learn more about the TESS mission at:
https://blogs.nasa.gov/tess/
You can learn about other NASA missions at:
https://www.nasa.gov/missions
You can learn more about Keivan Stassun's career and research projects at:
http://my.vanderbilt.edu/kstassun/
You can learn about Keivan Stassun's work on helping young people with autism become scientists at:
https://www.vanderbilt.edu/autismandinnovation/